The Railway Children

E. NESBIT

Level 2

Retold by Karen Holmes
Series Editors: Andy Hopkins and Jocelyn Potter

Pearson Education Limited
Edinburgh Gate, Harlow,
Essex CM20 2JE, England
and Associated Companies throughout the world.

ISBN: 978-1-4058-6964-5

The Railway Children was first published by Wells Gardner, Darton and Co. in 1906
This adaptation first published by Penguin Books Ltd 1995
Published by Addison Wesley Longman Ltd and Penguin Books Ltd 1998
First published by Penguin Books Ltd 1999
This edition first published 2008

5 7 9 10 8 6 4

Typeset by Graphicraft Ltd, Hong Kong
Set in 11/14pt Bembo
Printed in China
SWTC/04

Published by Pearson Education Ltd in association with
Penguin Books Ltd, both companies being subsidiaries of Pearson Plc

For a complete list of the titles available in the Penguin Readers series please write to your local
Pearson Longman office or to: Penguin Readers Marketing Department, Pearson Education,
Edinburgh Gate, Harlow, Essex CM20 2JE, England.

Contents

Introduction

'What did the men want, Mother?' she asked. 'Why are you crying? Is somebody dead?'

'No,' Mother said. 'Nobody is dead. I can't tell you . . .'

Roberta, Peter and Phyllis live happily in London with their parents. But on Peter's tenth birthday, some strange men come to the house. After that, the children's father isn't there. Where is he? When is he coming back?

The children and their mother do not have much money, so they move away from London to a smaller house.

Near their new home there is a railway line. The children quickly make new friends at the railway station and on the trains.

Then exciting things start to happen.

Edith Nesbit was born in London in 1858. Her father died when she was only four years old. After that, she went to different schools in England, France and Germany. She was a very beautiful woman but she was often unhappy. In 1880 she married Hubert Bland. They had three children. They didn't have much money and Edith worked hard. She wrote books and stories for money.

Edith took ideas for her stories from her life. In her book *The Story of the Treasure Seekers* (1899), the children look for money for their mother and father. *The Railway Children* (1906) is her most famous book. Edith lived by a railway when she was a young girl. So some of her life is in this book too. She died in 1924.

There was a film of *The Railway Children* in 1970. Jenny Agutter played Roberta. Thirty years later, Jenny was also in the television film of 2000. This time, she played Roberta's mother.

Chapter 1   Leaving the City

To begin with, they were no railway children. They looked at trains sometimes and they thought they were exciting, but they did not know anything about them.

There were three children. Roberta was the oldest and the most clever. Then there was a boy, Peter – he wanted to be the boss. Phyllis was the youngest.

They lived with their mother and father in a house near the city. They were lucky children. They had everything – pretty dresses, warm fires, good food.

Their mother played with them and told them stories and they often laughed. Their father was never angry with them and he was always ready to help them.

They were lucky and they were happy, and then . . .

It was Peter's tenth birthday. His mother and father gave him a train engine. Peter loved trains. When he left school he wanted to work on a train.

Peter loved his engine more than anything – then Phyllis broke it! Phyllis often broke things. Peter was very sad, but he knew that Father could put it together again.

When Father came home, he looked at the engine.

'I can repair it, but you must all help me.'

'The girls too?' Peter asked. He thought only boys could repair things.

'Girls are as clever as boys, you know,' Father said. 'Do you want to help us repair the engine, Roberta?'

'Yes, I want to help,' Roberta said. 'Do you think I can?'

Before Father could repair the engine, two men came to see him and Mother. The children could hear them talking. They were very angry.

The children heard the men leave the house. Later, Mother came back into the room. Her face was very white and her eyes were red from crying.

'Father is going away,' she said.

Roberta knew that something was wrong.

'What did the men want, Mother?' she asked. 'Why are you crying? Is somebody dead?'

'No,' Mother said. 'Nobody is dead. I can't tell you what is wrong.'

The children went to bed. Roberta could not sleep because she could hear her mother crying.

The next day Father was not there. Mother went out.

'There's something wrong,' Peter said.

It was very late when Mother came home. She was tired and sad.

'Listen to me,' Mother said. 'Father is not coming back for a long time. You must help me.'

'How can we help?' asked Roberta.

'You must be good and happy and you must not ask me any questions. All I can tell you is that Father is away because of his job.'

When they went to bed, Peter said, 'Let's start being good tomorrow morning.'

'Why not today?' Phyllis asked.

'Because it's late and there's nothing to be good about now,' Peter said.

Five days later Mother told them, 'We're leaving the city. We're going to live far away in a little white house. I know you're going to love it.'

They put everything in boxes – cups and plates, dresses and shoes, games and books.

'This is exciting,' Peter said. 'Can we move to a new house every month?'

'Listen to me,' Mother said. 'Father is not coming back for a
long time. You must help me.'

But Roberta saw her mother's sad face and knew that it was not a game.

The next day they went by train to their new house. It was late at night when they arrived.

They stood on the cold, dark station and watched the train leave them. They did not know then, standing there cold and afraid, how important the railway and the station were for them.

Chapter 2   Stop Thief!

They walked for a long time before they arrived at their new home.

Mother found the key and opened the door. Inside the house there was no fire and nobody to meet them. Phyllis wanted to cry.

'We must make a fire,' Mother said.

'I want Father,' Phyllis said. 'He can make fires.'

Roberta kicked her.

'Be quiet!' she said. Mother did not like talking about Father.

The next morning they looked at the house. It was small and quite dirty, but it was pretty.

'This house is prettier than our old house,' said Phyllis. 'Let's look at the garden.'

Below the house they could see the railway line and a dark tunnel. They could not see the station but they could see a big bridge.

All day they helped Mother in the house. Late in the afternoon, they went to look at the railway.

They stood next to the railway line. Suddenly they heard a noise and looked at the tunnel. Next minute a train came past them.

They stood on the cold, dark station and watched the train leave them.

'The engine is very big,' Peter said.

'Do you think the train is going to the city?' Roberta asked.

'Let's go to the station and ask,' Peter said.

Behind the station was a lot of coal.

The Station Master saw them and came to talk to them.

Peter asked, 'What's the coal for?'

'It makes the engine work so that it can pull the train,' said the Station Master.

There was a lot to do and see at their new home and they soon forgot their old house in the city.

In June it began to rain and the weather turned unusually cold.

'Mother,' Roberta said, 'can I make a fire?'

'No,' her mother said. 'We can't make fires in June because the coal is too expensive.'

With Father away, they did not have much money. They could not buy coal to make fires.

Then Peter had an idea.

'What's your idea?' the girls asked.

'I'm not telling you,' he said.

'Why not?' asked Roberta.

'I can't tell you what I'm going to do. It's dangerous. Don't tell Mother where I am, OK? Say you don't know.'

Peter went – the girls did not know where. The next day there was some coal in the coal-box and they made a fire. The coal came from the station. Peter brought only small bags of coal home so that Mother did not know about it.

One night Peter went back to the station to take some more coal. The girls followed him. That night the Station Master caught him. The two girls stood behind a tree and listened.

'You young thief!' the Station Master shouted.

'You young thief!' the Station Master shouted.

'I'm not a thief!' Peter answered.

'You, you are,' the Station Master said. He was very angry. 'You're taking coal from the railway. I'm taking you to the station.'

Roberta ran across to them.

'Not the *police* station!' she said. 'Please don't take him to the police station!'

'Oh, it's you – the children from the small house!' the Station Master said. 'Why are you taking this coal?'

'Because it's cold and Mother says coal is too expensive for us to have a fire.'

The Station Master smiled. 'You can go this time,' he said, 'but next time you must remember that this is railway coal. You cannot take it from the station or you *are* a thief.'

The children were very happy that they could go home. Again and again Peter said, 'I'm not a thief. It was not wrong to take some coal when there was a lot of it at the station.'

But they all knew that it *was* wrong.

Chapter 3   New Friends

The Station Master was their first friend at the railway. Their second new friend was Perks. He worked there, too. Their third new friend was an old man. They saw him every day on the train.

'Do you think he's going to the city?' Phyllis asked. 'Is he going to see Father? And when is Father going to write to us?'

'I don't know,' Roberta said. 'Let's all wave when the train goes past tomorrow. The train can take our love to Father.'

Every morning they waved at the train and every morning their new friend on the train waved back at them.

Every morning they waved at the train.

They often went to the station to talk to the Station Master and Perks. Perks told them stories about the trains and the Station Master was always happy to see them. He said nothing more about Peter and the coal.

One morning Mother was ill. That night she was worse, so Roberta called the doctor for her.

'She must stay in bed,' the doctor said. 'And she must stay warm. Give her good food to eat – a lot of meat and fruit.'

Roberta was afraid. Mother was very ill but they did not have any money to buy a lot of meat and fruit.

'What can we do?' she asked Peter and Phyllis.

'We must find somebody to help us,' Peter said.

The children thought for a long time before they thought of somebody.

'Perhaps the man on the train can help us,' Roberta said.

The next morning when the train went past their house, the old man saw a big piece of paper next to the railway line. It said: LOOK OUT AT THE STATION. When the train arrived at the station, he looked out of the window. Phyllis was there. She gave him a letter.

The letter said:

To Mr We Don't Know Your Name

Mother is ill. The Doctor says we must give her good food but we don't have any money because our father is in the city. Can you help us? We can pay you back later.

From Roberta, Peter and Phyllis.

Below their names they wrote down what they wanted for their mother.

That night Perks came to their house with a big box. Inside, there was a lot of food for everybody. There was a letter, too.

When the train arrived at the station, he looked out of the window. Phyllis was there. She gave him a letter.

Children,

I am happy to help you. Here is the food for your mother.

The old man's name was under that, but his writing was bad and they could not read it.

'Is Mother going to be angry when she knows about our letter to the old man, do you think?' Roberta said.

Two weeks later the children put up another big piece of paper near the railway line. It said: MOTHER IS MUCH BETTER. THANK YOU.

Mother did get better – and she was *very* angry about their letter to the old man on the train.

'You must never ask people for money!' she said.

Chapter 4 Danger on the Railway

Their best times of the day were when they went to the station to watch the trains and talk to Perks and the Station Master. They met Jim and Bill – they worked on the engines.

One morning when the children were near the tunnel, they heard a noise.

'What's that?' Phyllis asked.

The noise did not stop. It came from under their feet.

'Look at that tree,' Peter shouted. 'It's moving!'

They looked at the big tree near the tunnel. It moved slowly nearer and nearer to the railway line.

'The tree is walking!' Phyllis said.

'Trees can't walk,' said Peter.

More trees began to move.

'I don't like this,' Phyllis said. 'Let's go home.'

12

There was another noise and trees began to fall on the railway line.

'What can we do?' Roberta said. 'A train is going to come through the tunnel and hit the trees. There's going to be an accident!'

'We must stop the train,' Peter shouted. 'Quickly! We must wave at Jim and Bill and stop the train.'

'But we always wave at the train,' Roberta said. 'They're not going to stop when they see us waving at them.'

Peter had an idea. 'We must wave something red. Red is for danger.'

'Our skirts are red!' Roberta said.

'We can't wave those,' said Phyllis.

'We must! We must stop the train or there's going to be an accident!'

The girls took off their skirts. When the train came past they waved them and shouted 'Stop! Stop!'

'It isn't stopping! It isn't stopping!' Phyllis shouted – but then suddenly it did.

They ran up to the engine and told Jim and Bill about the trees on the railway line near the tunnel.

'You were very clever to wave those red skirts,' Jim said. 'When I saw those red skirts, I knew there was some danger on the line.'

Peter and Phyllis found it all very exciting, but Roberta did not. She knew that it was lucky that many people did not die. Sometimes at night she could not sleep when she remembered how afraid she was.

Chapter 5   Fire! Fire!

One of the children's best friends at the railway was Perks.

A few weeks after they stopped the train, Roberta said, 'It's Perks's birthday soon. He's always good to us. Perhaps we can do something for him.'

'But we have no money,' Phyllis said.

'Let's go down to the bridge at the river and catch some fish,' Peter said. 'We can think of something for Perks when we are fishing.'

They did not catch any fish, but they stayed near the river and watched the boats. These boats were small houses. Families lived on them.

A man came out of one of the boats and shouted at them.

'What are you doing? You can't fish here.'

'Why not?' Peter asked. 'We're not doing anything wrong.'

'Yes, you are,' the man said. 'You can't fish here!'

Roberta ran across and pulled Peter away before he started a fight.

After the man walked away, his wife spoke to the children.

'Please don't be angry with my husband,' she said to Peter. 'He usually likes children.'

The women and her husband lived on the boat with their baby. 'I'm going to find my husband,' she said.

'Is the baby OK on the boat without you there?' Roberta asked.

'Oh, yes,' the woman said. 'I'm only going away for a few minutes.'

The children stood on the bridge and watched the boat. It was quite dark now and they were tired. It was time to go home.

They stayed near the river and watched the boats.

Suddenly Phyllis shouted, 'Look! What's that?'

'The boat is on fire!' Peter said.

'The baby!' Roberta shouted. 'We must get the baby.'

They all ran to the boat. Peter pushed Roberta back.

'I'm going to find the baby,' he said. 'Stay here.' But Roberta did not want to wait.

Together they jumped on the boat. It was dark and there was a lot of smoke. They could not see, but when the baby began to cry, they quickly found him.

They climbed off the boat and Roberta ran to the village. 'I'm going to find the man and his wife,' she said.

She found them in a shop.

'Come quickly,' she said. 'Your boat is on fire.'

The woman began to cry. 'My baby! Where's my baby?'

'He is OK,' Roberta said. 'We took him off the boat.'

They all ran back to the boat. The man stopped the fire with water from the river.

'I'm sorry I was angry with you earlier,' he said. 'Because of you, our little boy is not dead! Thank you! Thank you!'

And the next day he took them down the river on his boat.

'You can catch fish here when you want to,' he said.

'We made a new friend today,' they told Mother when they went home.

'Now you have friends on the railway and friends on the river,' she said with a smile.

When Mother said 'railway', they remembered Perks's birthday.

'What are we going to do?' Roberta asked.

Together they jumped on the boat.

Chapter 6   A Village Birthday

Peter had the idea.

'Perks is always nice to everybody in the village. Perhaps a lot of people want to give him a gift for his birthday.'

They went to every house and every shop in the village. Most people wanted to give something for Perks.

The next day, when they knew Perks was down at the railway station, they took these gifts to his house. Mrs Perks opened the door.

'We know it's Mr Perks's birthday and we want him to have these,' Peter said, and showed her all the bags and boxes.

Mrs Perks began to cry.

'What's wrong?' Peter asked. He could not understand why she cried. Most people *liked* to get gifts on their birthday.

'I'm crying because I'm happy,' Mrs Perks said. 'All these new things! Food to eat, and something for Mr Perks to wear and games for the children.'

And she started to cry again.

But when Perks came home, he was not happy. He was very angry.

'Take these back!' he shouted. 'I don't want you to give me things.'

'Why not?' Peter asked. 'We always get gifts on our birthdays.'

'I can't take all this from you.' Perks said more quietly. He knew the children had no money to buy gifts.

'But it isn't all from us,' Roberta said. 'Everybody in the village wanted to give you something.'

Then she told him what all the people in the village said about him. 'You help people and you are their friend. That's why they gave us these things for you.'

Mrs Perks began to cry.

'You must take these gifts, Mr Perks,' Peter said, 'or everybody in the village is going to be very unhappy.'

Slowly, Perks began to smile.

'Well, I *must* take them, then,' he said. 'Thank you very much.'

And he asked the children into his house for tea.

Chapter 7   The Spy

When the children came to live in their new home, they talked about their father all the time but later they did not talk about him as much. Roberta thought that Mother was sad when they said his name.

'Is Father coming home one day?' she asked her mother.

'Yes he is, but not for a long time.'

Roberta knew that her father was not ill or dead, but she did not understand why he was not with them. Mother told them nothing. All she said was, 'One day he's going to come home and then we can all be happy together again.'

Most of the time the children were good. They did not fight because they knew Mother did not like it. But sometimes they forgot to be good.

One day Roberta and Peter had a big fight. They were in the garden and Peter took the garden knife from Roberta.

'I want that!' Roberta said.

'I want it, too!' Peter shouted and pulled it away from her.

Roberta pulled, too. Suddenly the knife went into Peter's foot. He started to cry.

'Stop crying,' Roberta said. 'You're not badly hurt.'

But he did not stop crying. Mother came out to see what all the noise was.

'Are you hurt, Peter?' she asked.

'It's my foot.'

One day Roberta and Peter had a big fight.

When Mother took off his shoes, there was a lot of blood on his foot.

Phyllis ran to get the doctor.

'Is Peter going to die, Mother?' Roberta asked, very afraid.

The doctor looked at Peter's foot.

'He's going to be OK, but he must stay in bed.'

Peter did not like staying in bed because he had nothing to do. Roberta went to the station and asked Perks for any old newspapers for Peter to read.

'Yes, girl, I have a lot of old newspapers,' Perks said. 'Take these.'

Roberta carried them home, and she looked at them. Suddenly she stopped and she read one newspaper story very carefully. When she finished, her face was white and sad.

There was the name of her father. 'Five years in prison,' the newspaper said. 'This man is a spy!'

Now she knew why Father did not come home. He was in prison!

'They are wrong,' she thought. 'My father isn't a bad man.'

Later she went to see her mother and showed her the newspaper.

'Oh, Roberta,' her mother said. 'Your father did not do anything wrong. Those two visitors in London were policemen. They thought Father was a spy after they found some letters. They took Father away.'

'But who *was* the spy?' Roberta asked.

'I don't know,' her mother said, 'but there was one man at your father's work – he didn't like Father. I think it was him.'

'What can we do?'

'We can only wait for Father to come home again.'

A week later Roberta wrote a letter. It was to the old man,

Suddenly Roberta stopped and she read one newspaper story very carefully.

their friend on the train. She cut the story out of the newspaper and sent it with her letter.

To my friend,

You see what it says in the newspaper about our father. But I know Father is not a spy. Someone put those papers and letters in Father's desk. Please help us to find the spy. Please, please help us.

Your friend, Roberta.

That afternoon she took the letter to the station. She gave it to the Station Master and asked him to give it to the old man the next day.

Chapter 8   Accident in the Tunnel

Next day, Peter got out of bed for the first time – his foot was better now. The children went to watch a game at the school. One boy ran in front and left pieces of paper behind him. The other boys followed the paper and tried to catch the first boy.

The first boy went near the railway line and into the tunnel. Soon the other boys followed.

Peter, Roberta and Phyllis watched. They saw the boys go into the tunnel. Then they ran as fast as they could to watch them come out of the tunnel again, near the station.

'Look, here they come,' Peter said.

The boys came out of the tunnel and ran away.

'There, that's all,' Roberta said. 'Now what are we going to do?'

'One boy is down there, in the tunnel,' Peter said. 'Six

24

went in but only five came out. We must go in and find him.'

They went into the tunnel to look for the boy.

Inside the tunnel it was very dark and cold and wet.

Phyllis was afraid. 'I don't like this,' she said. 'I want to go home.'

Then, before they could answer her, they heard a noise.

'It's a train!' Roberta said. 'What can we do?'

'Quick!' shouted Peter. 'Get down!' In no time they were all face-down on the floor of the tunnel, next to the railway lines.

The train came very near to them, then it was gone.

'We're OK, but that was very near!' Phyllis said. 'Where's the boy? Do you think he was on the railway line?'

They ran down the tunnel and soon they found the boy. He was down on the floor of the tunnel, next to the railway line. His eyes were closed.

'Is he dead?' Phyllis asked.

'No, he's not dead. The train didn't hit him.'

The boy opened his eyes.

'My leg,' he said. 'It hurts badly... Where did you come from?'

'We saw you go into the tunnel, but we didn't see you come out again,' Peter said. 'Can you walk? It's OK. We can take you out of the tunnel.'

But the boy could not walk.

'We must get help,' Roberta said. 'I'm going to stay with him. You go to the nearest house and get somebody to help us.'

'No,' Peter said. 'I'm staying with him. You go for help.'

Roberta stayed; Peter and Phyllis went to find help. Because she was the oldest, she thought she must stay with the boy. After they left she took off the boy's shoe. His leg was very badly hurt.

The boy opened his eyes again. 'What's your name?' he asked.

'Roberta.'

'I'm Jim.'

'My brother and sister are getting somebody to help you,' Roberta said. 'I wanted to stay with you.'

'That's good of you. It's very dark in here. Are you afraid?'

'No. Not – not much.'

'Take my hand,' Jim said. They sat together in the dark tunnel and waited for somebody to come.

Chapter 9   Help at Last

Peter and Phyllis walked a long way before they came out of the tunnel.

When they were outside, Phyllis said, 'I'm never going into a tunnel again.'

'We're going back into the tunnel to help that boy,' Peter said. 'We must.'

They ran to the nearest building. It was the signal-box. They called for the signalman but there was no answer.

They looked through the door. The signalman was in a chair in the corner, his eyes closed.

Peter shouted at the signalman; he opened his eyes.

The signalman was angry with them. He was afraid. He knew that it was wrong to sleep when he was at work.

'My son is ill,' he said. 'I sit with him at night and I don't sleep. Please don't tell anybody that you found me sleeping at work. I don't want to lose my job.'

'We're not going to tell anybody,' Peter said.

'But you must help us,' Phyllis said. 'There's a boy in the tunnel and he can't walk because he hurt his leg.'

The signalman was in a chair in a corner, his eyes closed.

'I can't help you. I must stay here. Run to the house up the road. There's somebody there most of the time.'

At the house they found two men. They all went back to the tunnel together, and they found Roberta and Jim.

Together they carried Jim back to their house and Mother called the doctor.

The doctor came and looked at Jim's leg.

'I want to watch,' Peter said. 'I want to see what the doctor is doing. Is there going to be a lot of blood?'

'Stop it!' Roberta said angrily. 'Jim's badly hurt. This isn't a game, you know.'

Mother wrote a letter to Jim's grandfather. She told him about the accident.

'Can Jim stay here?' Peter asked. 'I want another boy in the house. There are too many girls here.'

'We don't have much money,' Mother said. 'We can't buy him what he must have.'

The next day a man visited Mother. The children did not see him when he arrived because they were in the kitchen.

'Is it the doctor?' Phyllis asked.

'I don't think it is,' Peter said. He opened the kitchen door and listened to Mother and the man in the front room.

Then Mother called Roberta.

'Jim's grandfather is here,' she said. 'He wants to meet you.'

The children quickly washed their hands and faces and went to the front room.

Mother was in a chair near the window. In another chair near her was – the old man from the train!

'Oh! It's you!' Roberta said. Then she remembered to say hello.

'This is Jim's grandfather,' Mother said.

'Are you here to take Jim away?' Peter asked. 'Can he stay with us for a week or two?'

Mother was in a chair near the window. In another chair near her was – the old man from the train!

'Yes, he can come home when he's better,' said the old man.

Then he and Roberta walked through the garden together.

'I have your letter,' he said, 'and I think I can help you.'

Chapter 10   A Happy Day

Slowly Jim's leg got better. He and the children were good friends now. Every day they all had lessons with Mother and played games outside in the garden.

Because the children were with Jim all the time, they had no time to go to the railway.

'We never go there now,' Phyllis said.

'Let's go tomorrow,' Roberta said.

In the morning they ran down to the railway line.

'Wait for me!' Phyllis shouted.

The train went past and they all waved. Jim's grandfather waved back, and all the other people on the train waved, too. They all had newspapers in their hands and smiles on their faces.

'Why did they all wave?' Peter asked.

'I don't know,' Roberta said. 'Perhaps it was because of the old man.'

She was right. That morning the old man asked everybody on the train to wave when they saw Roberta, Peter and Phyllis.

The children went back to the house. Roberta could not think about her lessons. She was excited and afraid at the same time.

'Are you ill?' Mother asked.

'I don't think so,' Roberta said. 'But can I go outside, please? I don't want to be inside the house.'

Mother said Roberta could go outside. She walked slowly through the garden and down to the railway station.

On the road to the station people smiled at her and said hello.

The train went past and they all waved. Jim's grandfather waved back, and all the other people on the train waved, too.

'Daddy! My daddy!'

When she got to the station, the Station Master smiled too, then quickly walked away.

'Something's going to happen,' Roberta thought.

Perks came out. He had a newspaper in his hand.

'This is very good,' he said, waving the newspaper. 'Very, very good.'

'What is it?' Roberta asked.

Before he could answer, the train came into the station.

Then something very good and very exciting happened.

Only three people got out of the train. The first was an old lady. The second was a young lady, and the third –

'Daddy! My daddy!'

Everybody looked out of the windows of the train and saw the pretty girl run and throw her arms around the tall, thin man.

'This is my happiest day. I'm so happy you're home,' she said as they walked down the road to the house.

'They caught the spy,' her father said. 'Everybody knows now that I was not the spy.'

'I always knew that it was not you, Father. We all knew – Mother and I and Jim's grandfather.'

'Because he helped me, I'm now out of prison,' said her father. 'Now go into the house and tell your mother that I'm home.'

Roberta went into the house and spoke to her mother. Father stood in the garden, watched the birds and the flowers, and knew that now he was home. Home with his wife and his children. His railway children.

.

ACTIVITIES

Chapter 1

Before you read

1 Look at the Word List at the back of the book. Find any new words in your dictionary. Then put the right words in these sentences.

The (a) … broke a window and cut his hand. There was (b) … everywhere. The police caught him easily and he went to (c) … .

The train driver went through a red (d) … . He didn't know his train was in (e) … . Then he saw an (f) … on the (g) … in front of him. It turned off the line at the last minute. There was nearly a very bad accident. The driver was very (h) … .

2 Read the Introduction to the book and answer these questions.
  a Do the children live near the railway when the story begins?
  b The children's lives change in two big ways. What are they?
  c Did Edith have an easy life?

While you read

3 Answer *Yes* or *No* to these questions.
  a Does Peter's father repair the engine?   .....
  b Does the children's father leave with the two men?   .....
  c Does he come back?   .....
  d Is he going to the white house with the family?   .....
  e Does Mother really want to leave the city?   .....
  f Are they excited when they get off the train?   .....

After you read

4 Discuss these questions. What do you think?
  a The family are leaving the city and moving to the country. Which do you like better – the city or the country? Why?
  b Which of these things are most important for a child?
    birthday gifts   warm fires   nice clothes   happy parents
    good food   a nice house

Chapter 2

Before you read

5 What do you think?

    a Why will the railway station be important for the family?

    b Chapter 2 is 'Stop Thief!' Who will the thief be?

While you read

6 Which sentences are right? Tick (✓) them.

a	The new house is clean and pretty.	.....
b	It has a garden.	.....
c	They can see the railway station from the house.	.....
d	They can see a railway tunnel and a bridge from the house.	.....
e	They don't have money for coal.	.....
f	The children take coal from the station.	.....
g	The Station Master doesn't want to take Peter to the police.	.....
h	Peter doesn't think he's a thief.	.....

After you read

7 Work with another student. Have this conversation.
   Mother hears about Peter and the coal.

   Student A: You are Peter. You are sorry. You won't do it again.

   Student B: You are Mother. Are you angry or do you understand?

Chapters 3–4

Before you read

8 Discuss these questions. What do you think?

    a The children are going to make friends with an old man on the train. How will they make friends with him?

    b What dangerous things can happen on railway lines?

9 Read these sentences. <u>Underline</u> the right words in *italics*.

    a The children *get / don't get* letters from their father.

    b *Roberta / Mother* calls the doctor for *Roberta / Mother*.

    c The children write to the *Station Master / old man on the train.*

    d *Perks / The old man* gives the family a box of food.

    e Mother *is / isn't* angry when she hears about the letter.

    f The *ground / tunnel* moves under their feet.

    g The girls *take off / don't take off* their red skirts.

    h The driver *understands / doesn't understand* the red skirts.

After you read

10 Put these words in the right places in the newspaper story.

    fell   knew   live   ran   said   saw   saw   stopped   thought
    took   waved   were

    Railway Children Stop Accident

    Some trees (a) … onto the railway line yesterday. They (b) … between the tunnel and the station. Three children (c) … next to the line. They (d) … the danger. They (e) … very quickly. The girls (f) … off their red skirts. They (g) … there was a train on the way. They (h) … down the line. They (i) … their skirts at the train. The driver (j) … the skirts – red for danger! He (k) … the train. Everybody on the train (l) … 'thank you' to the railway children.

Chapters 5–6

Before you read

11 In the next chapter there is a fire, a boat and a baby. What do you think will happen? Talk to other students.

While you read

12 Finish the sentences with one word.

    a Families live on house boats on the ....

    b The children want to catch ....

    c The man shouts at the ....

    d The woman is sorry about her ....

    e She leaves her baby in the ....

    f Suddenly, the children see a ....

    g They find the baby inside the ....

    i They take the baby to its mother and ....

13 Write *likes* or *doesn't like* in the sentences.

    a Everybody in the village .... Perks.

    b Mrs Perks .... the gifts.

    c Perks .... the gifts at first.

    d Perks .... the gifts when he hears about the people in the village.

After you read

14 Think about these questions. Talk to other students.

    a Why does the man on the boat shout at the children?

    b Why does the woman leave her child on the boat?

    c Why does Mrs Perks cry when she sees the gifts?

    d Why doesn't Perks like the gifts?

Chapters 7–8

Before you read

15 What do you think?

    a Where is the children's father?

        * in prison   * in the city   * in another country

        * dead   * in hospital

    b What work does he do?

        * he's a spy   * he does important work for his country

        * he's a thief   * he cannot work because he is very ill

While you read

16 <u>Underline</u> the mistakes in these sentences. Write the right words.

    a The children never fight.   ....

    b Peter doesn't cry when the knife hurts him. ....

    c Peter is going to die.   ....

    d Perks reads about her father in a newspaper. ....

    e Roberta thinks her father is a bad man.   ....

f Roberta sends the newspaper story to the old man on the boat. ....

g Six boys go into the tunnel and seven come out. ....

h The children find two boys in the tunnel. ....

i The boy has a bad foot and can't walk out. ....

j Nobody stays with the boy in the tunnel. ....

After you read

17 Make sentences about the story. Use these words.

    a children's father / prison

    b police / letters and papers / desk

    c Now the police think / spy

    d children / try to help / boy / tunnel

    e they / in the tunnel / train comes through.

Chapters 9–10

Before you read

18 What do you think?

    a The boy knows one of the children's friends. Who will it be?

    b How is the story going to end?

While you read

19 Read the questions and write the names. Who …

    a doesn't want to go back in the tunnel? ....

    b is asleep when he is working? ....

    c is ill and doesn't sleep at night? ....

    d comes and looks at Jim's leg? ....

    e is Jim's grandfather? ....

    f stays with the railway children? ....

    g teaches the children every day? ....

    h waves to the children from the train? ....

    i smiles at Roberta at the station? ....

    j gets off the train at the station? ....

After you read

20 a The children help a lot of people in this story. Who do they help?

b They also do some bad things in the story. What bad things do they do?

Writing

21 The children's father is in prison but he is not the spy. He thinks about his family all the time. He writes to the children's mother. Write his letter.

22 The old man visits the children's father in prison. He tells him about the children. Father tells the old man that the wrong man is in prison. Write their conversation.

23 When Perks gets home, he tells Mrs Perks about the day. He saw the story in the newspaper. He saw the children's father get off the train. Mrs Perks wants to know everything. Write their conversation.

24 Roberta writes to the old man after her father comes home. She wants to say thank you. Write her letter.

25 There are many stories about trains and railway stations. Do you know one? Write about it.

26 The children's father is home now. How will the children's lives change? Write some ideas.

27 Which do you think is better: life in the city or life in the country. Write three good things and three bad things about each.

28 Take five words from the Word list at the back of the story. Write a story and use the five words.

Answers for the Activities in this book are available from the Penguin Readers website. A free Activity Worksheet is also available from the website. Activity Worksheets are part of the Penguin Teacher Support Programme, which also includes Progress Tests and Graded Reader Guidelines. For more information, please visit:
www.penguinreaders.com.

WORD LIST *with example sentences*

blood (n) There was a lot of *blood* from the cut on my hand.

coal (n) Put some more wood and *coal* on the fire.

danger (n) Planes aren't very *dangerous*. There's more *danger* on the roads.

engine (n) The *engine* pulled the train slowly up the hill.

gift (n) What *gifts* did you get on your birthday?

line (n) The train stopped because there was a dead animal on the *line*.

lucky (adj) You're *lucky*: you have a nice family and a good home.

must (v) We haven't got any food. We *must* get some.

piece (n) Write your answers on a *piece* of paper.

prison (n) He was in *prison* for 20 years because he killed somebody.

railway (n) We went to the *railway* station and got on a train.

repair (v) Somebody broke the window, so I'm *repairing* it.

signal (n) The s*ignal* was red, so the train stopped.
   Then the *signalman* changed it to green.

signal-box (n) The signalman looked out of the window of the *signal-box*.

spy (n) The *spy* found important information and sold it for money.

Station Master (n) The station worker didn't know, so he asked the *Station Master*.

thief (n) The *thief* took my money and ran away.

together (adv) They are good friends and they always sit *together*.

tunnel (n) It was dark when the train went through the *tunnel*.

wave (v) They *waved* their arms and shouted, 'Hello!'

A Christmas Carol
Charles Dickens

Scrooge is a cold, hard man. He loves money, and he doesn't like people. He really doesn't like Christmas. But then some ghosts visit him. They show him his past life, his life now, and a possible future. Will Scrooge learn from the ghosts? Can he change?

Fly Away Home
Patricia Hermes

Amy Alden finds a nest of goose eggs, but there isn't a mother goose. So she takes the eggs home. The baby geese think Amy is their mother. They follow her everywhere. But when the winter comes, they must fly south. Can Amy help them to fly away?

The Jungle Book
Rudyard Kipling

A family of wolves takes a little boy into their home in the jungle. The child learns and plays with the other cubs. But can he really live in the jungle? Will the other wolves want him to stay? And will the dangerous tiger Shere Khan catch him?

There are hundreds of Penguin Readers to choose from – world classics, film adaptations, modern-day crime and adventure, short stories, biographies, American classics, non-fiction, plays ...

For a complete list of all Penguin Readers titles, please contact your local Pearson Longman office or visit our website.

www.penguinreaders.com

Black Beauty
Anna Sewell

'Always be good, so people will love you. Always work hard and do your best.'

These were the words of Black Beauty's mother to her son when they lived with Farmer Grey. But when Black Beauty grew up and his life changed, this was sometimes very difficult for him. Not everybody was as kind as Farmer Grey.

The Prince and the Pauper
Mark Twain

Two babies are born on the same day in England. One boy is a prince and the other boy is from a very poor family. Ten years later, they change places for a game. But then the old king dies and they cannot change back. Will the poor boy be the new King of England?

Gulliver's Travels
Jonathan Swift

Gulliver travels across the sea from England and has an accident. He arrives in a country of very, very small people. What will they do with him? How will he talk to them? And why are the Big-enders fighting the Little-enders?

There are hundreds of Penguin Readers to choose from – world classics, film adaptations, modern-day crime and adventure, short stories, biographies, American classics, non-fiction, plays ...

For a complete list of all Penguin Readers titles, please contact your local Pearson Longman office or visit our website.

www.penguinreaders.com

Longman Dictionaries

Express yourself with confidence!

Longman has led the way in ELT dictionaries since 1935. We constantly talk to students and teachers around the world to find out what they need from a learner's dictionary.

Why choose a Longman dictionary?

Easy to understand

Longman invented the Defining Vocabulary – 2000 of the most common words which are used to write the definitions in our dictionaries. So Longman definitions are always clear and easy to understand.

Real, natural English

All Longman dictionaries contain natural examples taken from real-life that help explain the meaning of a word and show you how to use it in context.

Avoid common mistakes

Longman dictionaries are written specially for learners, and we make sure that you get all the help you need to avoid common mistakes. We analyse typical learners' mistakes and include notes on how to avoid them.

Innovative CD-ROMs

Longman are leaders in dictionary CD-ROM innovation. Did you know that a dictionary CD-ROM includes features to help improve your pronunciation, help you practice for exams and improve your writing skills?

For details of all Longman dictionaries, and to choose the one that's right for you, visit our website:

www.longman.com/dictionaries